HALLELUJAH
Poems and Prayers for
Fellow Travellers

And there shall be a highway, it shall be called the Way of Holiness. The unclean shall not pass over it; it shall become a pilgrim's way . . . Only the redeemed shall walk upon it, the ransomed of the Lord shall return. They shall enter Zion with singing and their heads shall be crowned with everlasting joy. Sorrow and sighing will flee away and gladness and joy will be theirs.

Isaiah 35:8-10

GW00721655

HALLELUJAH

Poems and Prayers for Fellow Travellers

Annette Garbett

ARTHUR H. STOCKWELL LTD.
Torrs Park   Ilfracombe   Devon
Established 1898
www.ahstockwell.co.uk

British Library Cataloguing-in-Publication Data.
A catalogue record for this book is available
from the British Library.

ISBN 0-7223-3756-6
ISBN 978-0-7223-3756-1
Printed in Great Britain by
Arthur H. Stockwell Ltd.
Torrs Park   Ilfracombe
Devon

Foreword

One dark November evening on the way home from School for Revival, held at Holy Trinity Church, Weston-super-Mare, I was still in a praise and worship state of being when the car and I were filled with the Holy Spirit. I was not sure I could continue driving and pulled over. Talking in tongues, maybe – but singing? That was something I'd not done before. I somehow made my way home. I cannot actually remember driving, but when I arrived I was definitely somewhere on cloud ninety-nine. A close encounter of the divine kind takes some time to get over – not that I am sure I have. After a lifetime of being a Christian it was to prove rather like falling in love all over again; I suddenly saw the world from a new perspective, although, in reality the world is still the same – or is it?

That night sleep was not really an option. I wanted to remain in that very loving embrace of Jesus. Up early the next morning, I felt as though I had been plugged into the universe; an ordinary walk with the dog did not seem a possibility as I wanted to run, jump and shout very loudly. I donned my walking boots and set off up and over the Mendips. Even the drizzle that morning seemed a very special gift.

Everything I looked at was truly alive that day and I felt a deep need to try and express it in words. Somehow they flowed – an unasked-for gift, which continues to flow months later. This poetry comes out of quiet times with God, pictures given, sermons and issues laid on my heart.

They are ideas that can perhaps take weeks to gel together or they can flow within a few hours. Partly, too, they also come from my love of words and their real meanings. Some things we know by heart; words, phrases from the Bible come easily to mind (or at least paraphrases) but have we really thought about or understood what something means?

My relaxation is in gardening and that includes its history, as well as that of the plants, apart from getting muddy in amongst the flower beds. To people living in the Middle Ages, who did not have the written word, many flowers had symbolic meanings; the message they gave was just as real as those we find in print. My garden in spring is full of many different coloured columbines, they were representative of the Holy Spirit. (The flower looks like a group of doves drinking from a fountain.) The name of the flower is derived from *columba*, the Latin for dove. It represents the works of the Holy Spirit and God's seven great gifts. This seems very appropriate; surely we should all feel an awareness, an overflowing of God's abundant gifts for us. No matter what our circumstances, if we walk in His way, there ought to be overflowing joy in our hearts. We should see the world from a different perspective – His.

Contents

Morning Walk	9
Window on a New Day	11
Evening Squall	12
Let the Light Shine	13
Morning Prayer	14
Separated	15
For David	16
The Key to Life	18
The Lord Is Our Shepherd	20
Anointed	22
Loving Totally	23
Thy Will Be Done	26
Raised to Life Eternal	28
For King and Country	29
Reflection	30
God's Symphony	31
God's Lifeboat	34
Worthless and Free	37
Chiselled for Eternity	38
Towards Zion	40
A Few Extra Thoughts	43

Morning Walk

Misty damp walk through wooded lanes,
Paths up hillsides between twisty, spent bracken and bramble,
Leaves soggy and slippery underfoot.
A carpet laid of
Burnished beaten copper
Dazzling the eye.
On up onto springy, tussocky grassland.
Drizzle sprinkled, mist enveloped, the only greenness close
In a shadowy world.
Walking high above the valley,
Looking down upon the spent quarry,
At shiny, granite table-slabbed rocks,
Then a shaft of bright light
Illumines the man-cut cliff side.
A path appears where none exists
Running down alongside the rock face,
A stream of water brightness
Where no river flows.
A trick of light in this damp glaucous world.
The path ventures on up into woodland.
A cathedral of uplifted naked branches
The bare ribs of this church allowing
Light to penetrate below,
Upon the verdigris canopy blown about my feet.

Whilst tree trunks, lit in silvery-grey armour
Stand sentinel,
Next to those in shaggy Lincoln-green overcoats.
The stones beneath mottled with crystalline lichen crusts
And all around the pervading fresh smell of watered earth,
With the gentle drip, drip of water off the last few tenacious leaves.
Then out onto the hilltop and there
In the stillness and calm of early morning
The only busyness a lolloping black dog,
Rushing hither and thither.
Sniffing early-morning scents, freshly laid.
Leaping forward to chase imaginary shadows,
Lost in his own moment of time,
Unseeing of the world below his never ceasing paws,
Nose to the ground,
Contented dogginess.

Whilst all I can do is stand,
Observant of the enveloping beauty of the noisy silence
Of a new day.
All of God's creation praising Him through its very existence,
In its time-honoured journey through season after season.
Have you heard the morning's Alleluia?

Window on a New Day

Opening the window onto a framed, arched cerulean sky
Watching as night passes into day.
The luminescent moon full
And in command, until the rising of the sun,
Lights and bathes the hills in a silvery grey.
Wispy tendrils of mist tree-curl in the dips and hollows,
Whilst naked trees raise twiggy hands heavenwards
Grisailled in silhouette against a lightening sky,
And just outside, one tree
Still retaining rustling leaves, shimmers russet brown,
Beneath, a candle lit for a new day.
A fiery berberis of rosy red and garnet hue,
The last vibrant shining of autumn.
Listen, the birds are fulsomely singing hymns of praise
Heralding the dawn.
Do we in the stillness of a new morning
Sing such tune-filled praise
To our Creator
Before the business and weariness of the day begins?
Do we freely give Him the glory?
Rejoicing
Before we lose ourselves in worldliness?

Evening Squall

The sky, afternoon early, darkening;
Low, flat altostratus cloud,
Blotting out all light, the last bright rays of autumn.
Gales forecast, storm clouds gathering,
Black on grey.
No longer do the last lights of the fading season
Cling to near bare branches.
Wind-tossed
Wind-blown
Into hurricane swirls, they pirouette
Until a sharper blast
Explodes them to diverse corners.
Then a lull, for all those glorious coloured leaves
To fall and lie sodden and lifeless,
Their final dance completed.
The ballet chorus has taken its final curtain.
Then overhead a honking and beating of wings on air
As passes over a skein of geese,
Low formation flying for immigrant flocks.
Winter heralded with strength and force,
The gusts grow stronger
Whipping round and through sentinel branches
Bending all before its powerful assault.
Finally in chilling needles the downpour,
The cloud becomes lowering mist
Wrapping itself into the landscape
Until all is wet and wet.
Parched earth drinks gratefully.
Whilst we, noses pressed to panes,
Prepare to sit out the darker months ahead.
Gentle nature sleeps
And above her an army of stronger, wilder forces
Marches.
Humankind watches,
For all his techno-advances
Winter elements still defy
And God-created seasons mark the passing of another year.

Let the Light Shine

Gazing upon winter flowering plants
Beyond the door,
And element-defying walls,
From sheltered warmth.
Nestled between silvery-grey, bushed thyme leaves,
Holding their scent close, without the kiss of sun
Are the tiny faces of the violas.
Night purple-black, velvet-textured
And luminous orange,
Shouting for joy.
Even though wind-whipped and torrent-washed
They have strength in their tininess
To survive the winter season's harsh reality.
No sun-drenched days of summer,
No balmy breeze
And yet,
They snuggle close and hold their heads up high.
Do you hear them
Yelling noisily,
When life feels drained of colour?
Do not yourself ebb away.
Live noisily,
Let the Light shine out,
Defy life's tribulations
And shout
Praise.

Morning Prayer

Dreamy sleep and comfy bed cockcrow disturbed
Light dawning, day renewed.
Heavenly Father, my morning prayer,
May I today have the strength to say
Thy will be done.
Lord let me not hear
That cockerel crow at my back,
As I deny Your presence.
Prepare me to take Your light into darkness.
Help me to understand, help me to hear,
To do Your bidding.
Guide me in Your grace and Your blessing
That broken in my weakness,
Spirit anointed,
Whatever You call me to,
I, in childlike trust,
Respond,
Copiously.

Lighter now, the cockerel, creation ordained, crows again.
Lord, I give You my today.

Separated

Gethsemane – fear of being alone,
Jesus,
Separate from God,
Soul's depth
Alone.
'Thy will, My Father'
Ever knowing,
Unable as yet to humanly comprehend –
Alone,
Yet
You relinquished Your power.
Soul barely anticipating
The complete, physical, mental,
Spiritual tearing apart of
Father and Son.
Then in humiliation, in pain,
In degradation
For love
Of Your children.
As body rent asunder,
So Temple curtain torn.
Your love so vast,
I, entering the Holy of Holies,
Approach the throne.
I am Your child
Resurrection gifted
I stand in royal robes
Cleansed by Your grace,
Unfathomable revelation
I love and trust in faith,
Feeling only a shadow of Your pain
In that garden
Of Gethsemane,
Suffered
For me.
Moment in time,
Friend deserted,
Your life's end beginning
Dawns first light
Of God's new eternal Heaven
As You stepped willingly
Into the unknown
For me.

For David

Beloved,
To arms called,
Prepare, make ready,
Victory in Christ is won.
Satan, wooden cross defeated,
Still defiantly hostile, fights for souls.
God commands His Church
Receive your battle orders.
Warrior for human lives
Come wage war 'gainst all the powers of darkness,
Rulers and authorities of evil.
Spirit led,
Gird your soul with prayer
That the panoply of God be yours.
Crusader for God's lost children
In Jesus trust.
Go forth,
Raise the banner,
Shout His battle cry.
Conquer
In His name.
Christian,
His soldier militant
Engage
Armoured by God,
Buckled within His truth,
Saturated in His Word,
Deny the devil's lies.
Heart protected,
Breastplate of righteousness clad,
Draw nearer to your God,
Justice and integrity be your watchword.

As a runner prepared to run the race
Fleet of foot, well shod,
So may your feet with readiness be fitted.
Go forth
Proclaim the Gospel of Peace.
Seek out new opportunities
To bring at rally cry
The Good News.
It is your defence.
In confidence trust your Saviour
Hold firm your shield of faith,
Lest arrows of doubt and temptation
Cause you to stumble and fall.
Upon your head
Wear the helmet of salvation,
Protection from the power and presence of sin.
Whilst in your right hand
The sword of the Spirit,
The Word of God to cleave your path
Against the enemy.
Give no ground,
Advance, always moving, yearning forwards,
That at last,
The good fight fought,
Battle-scarred and weary
Boasting only in Christ your King.
Rejoicing,
You come to Zion's hill.
Where awaiting her warrior,
Earnt in His name,
For love of the Father
You are blessed
With your crown of life and righteousness.

The Key to Life

Prodigal child,
Wandering wastrel,
Lost and alone,
Fearful,
Resisting,
Heart-hardened, confused.
In darkness hiding,
The Light of the World,
Eyes full with love
Stands at your door
And knocks.
You alone
Can bid Him enter.
You alone have the key
To open the door
To life everlasting
In Jesus.
Salvation secure,
Freely on bended knee
Accept Him.
Say the hardest words:
I am sorry, forgive me,
I accept You as Lord
Of my life.
Hand Him the key of your heart,
Ask Jesus to steward your life
As of Heaven.
His rule and authority
Be yours.

Prodigal child,
Repentant, returned
Feast your eyes upon Jesus,
Be filled with His Spirit,
Be fulfilled in your life.
In Him is your hope for the future.
Through Him
And to Him
Offer
A life full of service.
Ever talking, ever listening,
Always open,
Always learning,
Ever changing,
Ever growing
Closer to Him whom you serve.
Living in fullness
His purpose for you.
His only instruction,
Loving others as He loves.
Gather in His name,
Ask that His will might be done
For His kingdom.
Be constantly sharing
Your use
Of
God's given gift,
The key to your heart.

The Lord Is Our Shepherd

Children of the world
Scattered east to west,
As sheep across the hillside,
Shepherdless.
Sweet grass and herb starved
With rock strewn scrubland alone to graze,
Cliffs and precipices, no pastureland.
Some sheep higher and higher stray,
Searching.
In need of life-giving food,
Yet edging ever nearer death.
Needful of shepherd,
To call by name,
To guide, to care,
To love.

Lord Jesus, You came as shepherd,
Your true flock hear Your call
And
Gather to Your fold.
For those unheeding of the Shepherd's call,
Destruction, precipice fall.
For Your flock,
Caring Shepherd,
Loving Father,
A life eternal covenant
Offered in outstretched hand.
Your mark upon us, in awe of You,
We will speak no lies,
Have fear-free hearts
And singleness of action
In following our Shepherd King,
Who stands as banner
For those who rally to Him.

Faithful remnant,
Chosen generation,
Kingdom of believers,
Heirs of salvation.

Your Shepherd calls,
Your Shepherd leads
To pastures green
Nourished by springs of living waters.
Listen,
Hear Him,
He calls you by name.

Anointed

Golden oil of olives,
Precious fragrance scented,
Myrrh for suffering,
Cane, with hint of ginger warmth,
Cinnamon, sweet spice of kings,
Cassia for incense, priesthood used.
Holy of Holies drenching,
Consecrated to God.

Blood shed on mercy seat,
Jesus, Messiah
Anoints those who chose Him now
Through union with Him.

Christian eyes, oft tear-filled
Suffering through pain of life.
Loneliness and anguish,
Brokenness an offering.
Oh joyful heart
Who walks hand in hand with Christ,
Great High Priest,
Earth walked as man,
Sympathetic with our weakness.
Jesus, as dove anointed
In Jordan stood,
So we stand Holy Spirit anointed.
Life enhanced,
Inheritors of God's eternal plan.
Preordained to holy appointment,
Initiated into holy priesthood.
Mantle of wisdom covered,
Walk closely, heed His call,
Protect your anointing.
Life living reason, God's purpose,
A church of living stone.
United, standing in divine love,
White robe dressed, as perfume-scented bride,
Before His eternal throne.
Your fragrance, as holy cloud,
Surrounds, envelopes,
Declares us sacred,
Makes us accountable,
To walk in the Light of the King.

Loving Totally

Human being
Heart stamped 'created in Heaven,
Moulded in God's own likeness
Loved through all eternity,
Price paid on Calvary's tree'.

Are you empty space centred within,
Is there a heartfelt longing?
Unique design created,
Made in love
To worship and adore.
Hear your Father's voice,
Recognise your imperfections.
Ask forgiveness, it's freely given.
Price paid – remember.
Eternal life rewarded,
All He asks,
Love as I love you.

Are you prepared to walk the narrow path?
The nature that is you,
The self that is centred on you,
The clay that is you
Offer to your Creator.
Through His Spirit
Be remoulded in His likeness.
Love totally.

Be tranquil, do not let the storms of life
Stir you into futile action.
Quietly persevere, forbear,
Through endurance and hardship,
Through provocation or delay.
Be prepared to take the prolonged strain
Tolerating equally days of trial and disappointment
As days of joy, happiness and fulfilment.
Be self-possessed in waiting
Upon His will in all things,
Trusting and confident
That all things happen for love of you,
Willed by your Father for His greater purpose.
Learn patience.

Love totally,
Looking kindly upon His world
With His eyes,
Being careful to cause neither hurt
Nor inconvenience
But being gentle, affectionate,
Doing good actively and helpfully.
Giving freely, generously and abundantly
Of all that you have
And of all that you are.

Love totally
By being content
And never envious of others,
Believing that all that you have
Is all that you need.
Be not self-satisfied,
Make not the mistake of being blind to your own faults
Then condemning them in others.
Relinquish all traits of
Aggressiveness and being overbearing.
Be not boastful
Nor proud in anything
Except in your heavenly Father.

Love totally
By being not rude nor offensive,
Nor impolite.
Neither self-seeking,
Always putting others before yourself.
Be slow to anger,
Let no furious rage disturb a quiet temperament.
Keep no record of any wrong,
Nor stored resentments of other's actions and words.
Do not delight in evil,
Or those things that are harmful
To the goodness of the soul.
Keep no grudges, utter no slander,
Harbour no ill will
No spite or wrongful intentions.

In loving totally walk always in truth
In accordance with God's will,
Be upright, loyal and faithful
Towards your heavenly Father.
Protest and defend, overseeing
With constant vigilance yourself, your faith,
Your Christian brothers and sisters
And those as yet unborn in Christ.

Trust always in your faith in your Father God,
Upon His reliability, His truth and His strength
To defend you, to protect and to provide.
Look forward with confident expectation
In your inheritance in Him.
Hope always, longing, praying,
Entreating for His Kingdom to come,
Here on earth as in Heaven.

Persevere always, running the race of life,
Eyes upon your goal.
Continue steadfastly, unwavering to the last.
Resolute and determined
To complete your own Heaven-set life task
Using your God-given gifts
In His service.
Then in loving Him,
Always strengthened
In your love of the Redeemer,
Encouraged by His Spirit
You will not fail
And His love will be complete in you.

Let the Potter mould you
Completing the creation He saw in you
From the beginning.
Give away your heart,
Then as shining light
You will shine out for Him.

Thy Will Be Done

Have I faith enough?
Does every fibre of my being,
To soul's deepest depths
Believe
That with eyes upon Jesus firmly fixed
I can step out of the boat?
Amidst life's turbulence
When black thunder clouds roll in,
During the darkest watches of the night,
Wind howling and blowing,
Whipping up the waves,
In the fear that I feel,
Within the storm-tossed boat
Can I believe
I can water-walk
Into His outstretched arms?
Can I look deeply into His eyes
Believing the impossible
Is achievable
With His encouragement and belief
In me.

Have I faith enough
To believe that my prayers
Petitioned
Interceding.

Requests spoken and unspoken
From Your heart to mine
And from my heart to Yours,
Will, divinely, be met,
When praying in Your name
'Thy will be done.'
In a tired and weary world
Its own desire
For self,
Your call drowned out of daily lives,
A people plumb line tested
Heavenly standards failing
Give me today the burden and the passion to care
For You.

May I have faith enough
To leave the boat.
May I, through Holy Spirit power,
Pray
And believe my prayers
Are new foundation building
In Your world.
That Your new Jerusalem
Will be built within the hearts of men.

Raised to Life Eternal

Do we a lifetime spend in thrall to death,
Or do we in Christ
Vanquished
Live defiant over man's last enemy?
Salvation inheritors of God's Kingdom,
Followers in Christ's footsteps
Where'er we go.
Even through death's despair
Jesus has gone before,
Path prepared.
So through the valley
Passing,
Angel-accompanied,
Safe passage assured
So shall we come to eternal rest
From earthly labour.

As seeds from the harvest,
Sown in dishonour, raised in glory,
Sown in weakness, raised in power,
Sown in natural body form,
In death raised to spiritual life.
Mortal
To immortality.
Death has no victory
In Jesus our risen Lord.

In my passing
Let there be only gladness, joy and hopefulness.
Mourners, Jesus comforted,
Praise and do not despair
I am safely home.

For King and Country

Opening heavy oaken doors into the cool of centuries-old stone,
Patina-polished wood of hand-worn pew.
Myriad rainbow colours, sunlight dancing
Through storytelling glass.
The air fragrant with lovingly arranged lilies.
Overhead the vaulted arch of gold and azure-blue ceiling
Statue angel guarded.
In the poignant silence,
The church made holy
With timeless prayer and praise.
God is.

From font to craftsman-carved monument
Evidence of man's lifetime walk.
Upon the wall a memorial to life given
In the heat of battle,
Through pain, discomfort, fear
And belief in what is right and true.
To those who gave their greatest gift to fellow man.
Etched for king and country.

Is this a church living in You, Lord?
Are they Sunday parishioners
Offering their weekly strains and stresses,
To be comforted
In communion with a distant God?
Or are they living stones for Your Church,
Out in the world,
Missionaries vocationally called
For their King?
Ambassadors for a country
They have not seen,
But which has life in their hearts
Through faith.
Are they commissioned?
Walking, working, living
Amongst,
Beside
The lost and the lonely,
As a light in a dark world,
In thought and word and deed,
Proclaiming,
Jesus lives.

Reflection

Warm, still evening,
Summer's breath turning autumnal.
Lakeside air of tranquillity, naught
Save the sound of evening bird call.
The water rippled only by upturning ducks,
Deep-weed seeking for supper nourishment.
The trees at water's edge
Dipping low their branches
Hiding marginal banks
And sweeping the beaches of heat-dried, cracked mud.
There wading on furthest shore,
Stately, stepping out of shade, upright walks a heron.
Slowly, stalking fishy prey,
Pausing, waiting.
Then seemingly satiated, slowly takes to flight.
Gracefully,
Silently winged into wood,
Only to return shortly
Mate-accompanied.
They stand perfectly mirrored,
In evening sunlight,
Within deep viridescent glass.

Heavenly Father, as the water so reflects, may I reflect
You
In my heart.
In turning to You,
Through Temple veil-torn triumph
Of Jesus' love for me
May I
Spirit-filled and Spirit-transformed,
With unveiled face, so reflect
Your glory
In a needful world.

God's Symphony

Imagine sacred music, beyond imagining.
Perchance an echo may be heard
Within your Bible pages,
And sometimes, when expected least,
In drawing close to God
You loudly hear His music,
God's musical life accompaniment
Playing in your soul.

In the beginning
God created,
He saw all that He had made
And it was very good.

Can you hear creation's music,
The opening notes of God's overture?
First the prelude,
Three great themes
Rising and falling together,
Then the opening bars of the first movement.
Not the sound of gentle waves lapping upon the shore,
But the sounds of crashing,
Wave upon wave
Of surging energy
Pent-up,
Released
Into the sweet sound of heavenly creativity.
The harmony and lyrics,
The joy,
Of God's opus, newly begun.
The sun, moon and stars,
Land, sea and air;
All living creatures
And plants therein.
For each a new sound
As played by instruments never heard,
Swelling to crescendo upon crescendo,
Only to never reach its expected conclusion.

Discordant notes invade,
Beginning a fourth, but minor theme
At odds with God's harmonious tune,
Yet somehow used for the good of the whole,
So it remains entwined
As man, Satan encouraged,
Tries to write his own symphony within a symphony.

Then comes the second shorter movement,
For the whole composition, pivotal,
Highlighting the second, original, triune theme.

God so loved the world He gave His only Son.

This theme heralded by angelic voices,
More beautiful, more sweet,
Echoing and deepening
God's opening tune
A recapitulation of a creation begun in love,
Now with redemption interwoven.
Is it only to end upon discordant theme
With loud clashing tymphonic notes?
No, they are foreshortened,
The music becomes more passionate now,
Sweeter still,
Rising, as in creation's story,
Crescendo upon crescendo,
Soaring ever upwards
Until it ends
In pure heavenly sound.
Jesus,
Satan and death defeated,
Victorious reigns.

You will receive power
When the Holy Spirit comes upon you
And you will be my witnesses
To the ends of the earth.

And then the third movement,
The third variation of the triune,
Entering on notes of wind and fire.
A theme of sacredness,
Of harmony with whole, continues and swells.

Now newer instruments,
New chords and composition
With anthem voices raised.
Each unique to Christ's congregation,
His Church, Spirit-guided.
Darker themes still interweave
Through lighter moments,
God's dance, created at the dawn of time,
Never ceasing
Plays on
In the praises and prayers of His people.
Do you hear the notes you have been called to play?
Do you recognise where the great Conductor will lead?
Your part ordained,
Join the orchestra,
Play your love song.
Do not miss your introduction,
Keep your eyes upon the Composer.

This movement as yet unfinished
For human ear to hear.
Only as it plays is the composition heard,
By God's angelic host,
Rejoicing as lost children seek their part.

God alone has score-written
The fourth and final part
When a new song will be sung
In pure harmonious light,
Heralded with trumpet call
And pure angelic voices.
Earth-shaking music will play,
As all instruments
And singers
Praise.
God's sacred work,
His music absolute,
As in the sound of rushing waters or peals of thunder,
At the dawn of that new day
Will be completed,
And will fill the heavens, eternally.

God's Lifeboat

Aerial acrobatics of seagulls in flight
Over deep water,
Whilst screeching and squawking,
Quarrelling overhead.
As always
There is just one gull
Gliding higher,
Swooping faster,
Out-soaring the flock.
White aerodynamic loops and rolls
Against a steely-grey lowering, stormy sky,
Sunlit glistening,
Whilst behind
A coloured bow arches the heavens.

God remembering His covenant
Between Himself and all living creatures.

For You, Lord, there is always one,
A child of Yours with a true heart,
Listening,
Obeying.
Noah, prepared to give a lifetime
To constructing the unimaginable,
A desert-built boat,
Designed to godly specifications.
Faithful, believing and trusting,

Medieval master craftsman,
Noah's story symbolically read,
In their faith,
The nave designed.
From great arched cathedral
To small country church
Vessels, ships for God's children
To bring them safely home.

Lord, You continue to send out
A rescue mission,
Your boat, Your Church,
For those shipwrecked on life's seas.
How far into stormy waters are we prepared to sail?
When waves are overwhelming,
Are we still willing to go,
Without hesitation?
Even when there is danger of being broken upon the rocks
Do we set forth, trusting always in Your guiding hand?
Ever being sent, where, humanly, fear takes control.
Do we have faith enough to believe,
In the face of danger
Or shipwreck,
There are those needing rescue
And we alone can set sail?

Are we too afraid,
Prepared only to sail in calm seas, shore-protected,
Looking only for those a little out of their depth?
Or leaving harbour safety,
Navigating into the teeth of the wind,
Heedful of the cries of those that are drowning
In the churning water around us,
Will we head out into the gale.
Knowing You are at the helm?
To offer outstretched arms,
To pull aboard those drowning
In poverty, sickness, immorality,
Despair, selfishness, loneliness,
Hatred, fear or anguish.

The world needs Your lifeboat, Lord.
Jesus' cross, placed over rainbow,
New covenant of love and salvation,
By Your saving grace,
Offered freely.
Saviour commanded
Take the lifeboat out,
Under stormy skies,
Beyond land's safety and sight.
To offer the lifeline of rescue
To offer comfort in the safety of His arms,
To clothe in heavenly garments,
In the assurance of eternal life,
In His name.

Hear the seagulls cry,
Wake of ship following,
Are you ready to be one of those believing,
Listening,
Obeying and trusting?

Are you sailing far from land in a storm?
Unfearing of safety,
On watch for another lost soul
In need of a home-harbour-sailing lifeboat.

Worthless and Free

God said to Moses,
"Make a sanctuary and I will dwell among you."

Sanctuary of God
Dwelling amongst His chosen people.
Tent of the meeting
Tabernacle of Yahweh.
Table-fronted,
For bread of the Presence.
For each tribe of Israel
A loaf,
Always residing within sight of the Lord.
Sabbath renewed,
Saved for the priesthood,
Bread of life.

Christian,
Life given to Jesus,
A temple for His indwelling.
Ordained to the priesthood,
Enter now beyond the veil,
Good Friday rent,
In remembrance.
A place at the Lord's table.
His body, our bread, broken for us.
Fruit of the vine,
His lifeblood of sacrifice,
Cup of the new covenant.

I, worthless,
A sinner
Loved and invited,
Come to the feast
In His Presence.
I, abiding in Him,
Am free.

Chiselled for Eternity

Eyes
Love-filled,
Bruised, battered, bloodied,
Look down
From cross-beam height
Upon those who seek,
Those hearing,
Love me
As I love.

By grace and redemption
Saved.
God speaks,
Heart into heart.
Sculptor of your life,
With patience,
Creator skill and expectation,
Modelling,
Seeing your future perfection
As a light in the darkness.
Painfully,
Chiselling
At present flaws.
Life wounded,
Yet gift imparted,
Through human confusion,
Brokenness, desolation,
He sees the beauty of completion,
A lifetime's work of creation,
Crafted for eternity.

Through pain of design,
Compassion-filled,
Able to love
As He loves,
Seeing into others' souls,
Knowing the why.
Charged with the Holy Spirit's life breath
His sculpture,
Mirror imaged,
Spiritually,
Upon Him.
The eternal Creator,
In you,
Attains His perfection.
His child
Prepared for everlasting praise.

Towards Zion

Lord,
Move me,
Through knowledge of You,
To change my perspective
On life.
To see through Your eyes,
Through grace,
Bestowed on me,
In Jesus' name.
As I grow
In my understanding of You,
Let me be
Your hands and feet.
Always active
In faith,
In the position of influence,
Granted to me,
To change,
This world,
For You.

Lord, fill me,
So that every waking moment
Is occupied
Completely
In serving You.
May I,
Holy Spirit saturated,
Become Your whole creation
In Your abiding love
For me.

Lord, possess me,
So that,
Owned, totally,
By the price of Jesus' love,
I find nourishment
In You.

Thus anchored securely in You,
May I go forth in this world,
In the full assurance of my faith,
To encourage fellow-travellers.
To spur on those
Who walk, whether today or tomorrow,
Your highway.
Fearlessly,
With sincere heart,
Sure in the knowledge
We tread
Towards
Zion.

A Few Extra Thoughts
(With Bible Quotations)

Morning Walk
On that first morning of life being seen completely anew, the world appeared to be a hymn of praise, something that perhaps we lose in our modern busy world. If only we took time to stand and listen occasionally we could hear God in His creation as well as see Him in the world that surrounds us. Do we take time to stand and listen, to just be in God's presence? The psalmist knew all too well the awesomeness of God's creation and it is something in which we can all share.
(Psalm 19:1-4; 104; 148)

Window on a New Day and Evening Squall
And so it continued, everything – sights, sounds and colours – seemed more intense than before. God is good. Can we say the same when the weather is 'out of control'? Even adverse weather is part of God's creation; it is we in our comfort zone that find it difficult to cope with, particularly when we cannot tame or control it and we are at the mercy of the elements. When it is wreaking havoc and destruction we may have some idea of the awful, majestic power of God, who, in this day and age, we would also like to tame and put in a box. We all have various labels to put on that box but not many would suggest today that He is the power, the energy, the source of creation.
(Job 36:22-37)

Let the Light Shine

What I have really learnt in the last few years, more than ever before, is that when life seems really tough, when things don't seem to be happening as you want, hang on, sometimes by your fingertips, because then God is about His business. There is a reason. Believe, have faith, accept and shout praises very loudly. It does help. If you are only just hanging on, then be assured. God is creating in you something far greater – the person He knows you can be. If you are fighting it and doing things your way, He is not in control.
(Job; Acts 16:22-40; Hebrews 13:15)

Morning Prayer

I think a sermon of Richard's first stirred this thought one Sunday. I had been woken early by our local trio of cockerels, each one competing to make the loudest noise. One of them actually sounds as though he is being strangled; it made me think that that is often how we sound as we find it difficult to share our faith. How often in very simple words and actions each day do we neglect to give of ourselves, and fail to include Jesus in what we think and say and do? How often do we fail to be His hands, His feet, His eyes and ears, His caring heart as we spend our days amongst all those whose lives we touch? This surely is all denial.
(Matthew 26:69-75; 1 John 3:16-20)

Separated

This came from a very real and poignant feeling, that I still carry with me, that grew from that God encounter back in November. I can only begin to describe it as a constant ache. If you have seen Mel Gibson's film, *The Passion of the Christ*, then you are only too aware of the horrific torture and death of Jesus, but it is purely the physical that is depicted. What gives that feeling of sheer terror, though, is the complete desolation Jesus must have experienced in choosing to separate Himself from His Father. If you have ever stared into, or been enveloped in that 'black hole' that comes with real depression and feelings of being totally alone, then perhaps you have an echo of what He must have felt. Can most of us, though, even begin to imagine what He did, and He did it because He loves us.
(Matthew 26:36-46; Hebrews 6:19-20; 8)

For David

David, my eldest son, was always the swashbuckling type, from childhood play to wanting a career in the forces. Then he discovered Tolkien and he would have happily been renamed Aragorn, but by now he had given his heart to Jesus. His name in Hebrew does mean beloved of God, and it seemed appropriate to write this for him. We are all called to battle but we do not go unprepared. David can still wield his sword and wear the armour, but now it is of the spiritual kind for an even greater battle and for the supreme Commander – a battle where we already know the outcome, but a battle nonetheless, because, in Jesus, we have the victory.

(Ephesians 6:10-18; 1 John 5:1-5)

The Key to Life

The prodigal children of God's Church have recently been very much in our hearts and in our prayers. We had a special morning of prayer for the prodigals one Sunday, and Gerry had a picture of us at the feast and of having to go out and fetch those who were not there with us. That same day, Jenny preached on four keys to a fulfilled Christian life. I had also had a quest going for a while on the meaning of keys in the Bible. It had begun when reading that key in Hebrew means opener, in Greek it means something that shuts. This somehow seemed significant. Jesus also holds the keys of Heaven as head steward, not doorkeeper. Somewhere this all flowed together during the hours when most people sleep.

(Luke 11:5-13; 15:11-32; Revelation 3:7)

The Lord Is Our Shepherd

Several sermons started this train of thought, as well as a picture I had of sheep scattered across a hillside. God wants His sheep rounded up and they need to hear His voice. A phrase came to mind, that from a faithful remnant shall come a powerful people.

(Psalm 23, 100; Micah 2:12-13; Zechariah 13:7; Matthew 18:10-14; 26:31; John 10:1-16; Hebrews 13:20; 1 Peter 2:25)

Anointed

This poem flowed from a sermon on anointing. Hebrew brides are perfumed with a similar scent to that fragrancing the sacred Temple oil (there is a slight variation in ingredients), and there are those who have experienced the fragrance of God's Presence during worship.
(Exodus 30:22-33; 2 Colossians 1:21; 1 John 2:20, 27)

Loving Totally

A short phrase that we probably know by heart: have you ever taken it apart and thought about those words? It suddenly becomes more than just words, it becomes a Holy Spirit-filled way of living.
(1 Corinthians 13)

Thy Will Be Done

Do I have faith enough to believe that I can make a difference? Do I believe enough that even when filled with fear, for whatever reason, usually based upon the human feelings of pride and self-esteem, I can complete the task God is asking me to do? Do I also believe that even my prayers are changing the world for the betterment of His Kingdom? If we want Revival within the Church then we have to believe that what we do individually also has an impact even if we do not know what influence it is having within God's 'whole world' purpose. I had a picture of the buildings of Weston being demolished; the whole town appeared as a building site. There was dust everywhere as buildings were razed, but when the dust cleared, although initially unseen, the foundations of new buildings were being laid. Our prayers are influencing the lives of those we pray for even if, as yet, we do not see results that we can identify. In changing lives we also influence and further His Kingdom. All we need is faith.
(Matthew 14:22-34; John 6:16-22; Isaiah 28:16)

Raised to Life Eternal

We never have to experience anything that Jesus has not felt or understood from a human perspective. He knew the sorrow at the death of a loved one and He went through death for us, so even in our darkest moments, in the shadow of the valley of death, whether for those close to us, or for ourselves, we are never alone. This poem first stirred at the funeral of a loved teenage friend of my son, Christopher, and, afterwards, in talking about our faith and hope in a life to come. I was also reading a book about angels by Billy Graham at the time. We are always in these moments surrounded and guarded by angels.

(Psalm 23; Matthew 18:10; Romans 14:7-8; 2 Corinthians 5-8; 2 Timothy 4:7-8; Hebrews 1:14)

For King and Country

One Sunday morning, whilst visiting my sister, Katy, we went to her church. The war-memorial plaque was on the wall above my head and in one of those moments when you feel God speaking quite clearly, I wrote down several lines about serving our heavenly King and about being ambassadors for Him. It was only as the sermon progressed that it was apparent that I had already written down the main message of that morning. Sometimes God very clearly has something to say. Are we listening?

(John 18:36; 2 Corinthians 5:16-21)

Reflection

Sometimes God uses the things around us to speak a message into our hearts. This was a perfect still summer evening and it was one of those special moments of closeness with the Father when you offer up a prayer of thanks.

(2 Corinthians 3:7-18)

God's Symphony

This was a poem months in creation. I'd discovered all sorts of things about symphonies, trying to put the whole of God's story into words. Perhaps it was from that first morning in November when, even in early-morning silence, I could 'hear' creation's music. Words for sounds need a lot of imagination but, perhaps, this poem conveys just a little of what I was feeling. Simply read the Bible from Genesis to Revelation to understand.

God's Lifeboat
Watching seagulls diving in front of a rainbow, coming together with a sermon of Claude's led a whole train of thought to this poem.
(Hebrews 8-10)

Worthless and Free
From the old covenant of the Old Testament to the new covenant in Jesus, there is continuity in God's provision, from the bread in the Tent of the Meeting to the meal we share in remembrance of Jesus. When I actually come to take that communion meal, though, what is important is so simple – I am worthless and unclean, yet Jesus loves me, and, through redemption and my love for Him, I have my freedom.
(Exodus 40:22-23; Jeremiah 31:31-34; John 6:25-59)

Chiselled for Eternity
I was trying to watch the film, *Shadowlands,* about the life of C. S. Lewis, but kept getting disturbed. Every time I came back to the television he seemed to be saying the same thing: "Life is painful, but it is how we learn, both to be loved by God and how to love others." Thinking about this, it seemed very profound. We can only learn to love like God if we are changed, often in a way that is painful to us, by a caring loving Father who sees our potential, if only we will let go and trust in His training. We should be able to accept that it is part of our Christian growing-up.
(Proverbs 3:11-12: Isaiah 64:8: Hebrews 12:1-13: 2 Timothy 3:12-17)

Towards Zion
I really wanted just a few words to finish this collection of poems. I had scribbled lots of different thoughts, which I might use elsewhere in the future, but what I wanted was completion on the thought of fellow-travellers on God's highway. The final part of the missing puzzle (and this was how a lot of the poems have grown) was given to me by David sitting over a McDonald's meal as he told me of the sermon I'd missed the previous Sunday.
(Isaiah 60; Hebrews 6:19; 12:22-28, 13:6; Revelations 14:1)